MW00748475

WILLIAM SHAKESPEARE

Quotations

JARROLD|
publishing

SCENE FROM 'AS YOU LIKE IT'
Daniel Maclise 1806–1870

All the world's a stage,
    And all the men and women merely players;
They have their exits and their entrances;
    And one man in his time plays many parts,
His acts being seven ages. At first the infant,

Mewling and puking in the nurse's arms;
Then the whining school-boy, with his satchel
  And shining morning face, creeping like snail
Unwillingly to school. And then the lover,
  Sighing like furnace, with a woeful ballad
Made to his mistress' eyebrow. Then a soldier,
  Full of strange oaths, and bearded like the pard,
Jealous in honour, sudden and quick in quarrel,
  Seeking the bubble reputation
Even in the cannon's mouth. And then the justice,
  In fair round belly with capon lin'd,
With eyes severe and beard of formal cut,
  Full of wise saws and modern instances;
And so he plays his part. The sixth age shifts
  Into the lean and slipper'd pantaloon,
With spectacles on nose and pouch on side,
  His youthful hose, well sav'd, a world too wide
For his shrunk shank; and his big manly voice,
  Turning again toward childish treble, pipes
And whistles in his sound. Last scene of all,
  That ends this strange eventful history,
Is second childishness and mere oblivion;
  Sans teeth, sans eyes, sans taste, sans every thing.

AS YOU LIKE IT, ACT 2, SC. 7

O, beware, my lord, of jealousy;
It is the green-ey'd monster which doth mock
The meat it feeds on.

OTHELLO, THE MOOR OF VENICE, ACT 3, SC. 3

A jest's prosperity lies in the ear
Of him that hears it, never in the tongue
Of him that makes it.

LOVE'S LABOUR'S LOST, ACT 5, SC. 2

From forth the fatal loins of these two foes
A pair of star-cross'd lovers take their life.

ROMEO AND JULIET, PROLOGUE

OTHELLO AND DESDEMONA
Robert Alexander Hillingford 1825–1904

MARIANA IN THE MOATED GRANGE
Sir John Everett Millais 1829–1896

Teach not thy lip such scorn, for it was made
For kissing, lady, not for such contempt.

KING RICHARD THE THIRD, ACT 1 SC. 2

Is this her fault or mine?
The tempter or the tempted, who sins most?

MEASURE FOR MEASURE, ACT 2 SC. 2

Achilles...who wears his wit in his belly,
and his guts in his head.

TROILUS AND CRESSIDA, ACT 1, SC. 1

'Tis but thy name that is my enemy;
　　Thou art thyself, though not a Montague.
What's Montague? It is nor hand, nor foot,
　　Nor arm, nor face, nor any other part
Belonging to a man. O, be some other name!
　　What's in a name? That which we call a rose
By any other name would smell as sweet;
　　So Romeo would, were he not Romeo call'd
Retain that dear perfection which he owes
　　Without that title. Romeo, doff thy name;
And for thy name, which is no part of thee,
　　Take all myself.

ROMEO AND JULIET, ACT 2, SC. 2

ROMEO AND JULIET, ACT V SCENE 4
William Hatherell 1855–1928

SHAKESPEARE AND HIS FRIENDS
John Faed 1820–1902

No longer mourn for me
   when I am dead
Than you shall hear the surly sullen bell
Give warning to the world that I am fled
From this vile world, with vilest
      worms to dwell.
Nay, if you read this line, remember not
The hand that writ it; for I love you so,
That I in your sweet thoughts
      would be forgot,
If thinking on me then should
      make your woe.
O, if, I say, you look upon this verse,
When I perhaps compounded am with clay,
Do not so much as my poor name rehearse,
But let your love even with my life decay;
Lest the wise world should look
      into your moan,
And mock you with me after I am gone.

SONNET LXXI

O God! methinks it were a happy life,
To be no better than a homely swain;
To sit upon a hill, as I do now,
To carve out dials, quaintly, point by point,
Thereby to see the minutes how they run,
How many make the hour full complete;
How many hours bring about the day;
How many days will finish up the year;
How many years a mortal man may live.

KING HENRY THE SIXTH,
PART 3, ACT 2, SC. 5

*L*ove is blind, and lovers cannot see
The pretty follies that themselves commit.

THE MERCHANT OF VENICE, ACT 2, SC. 6

I AM NEVER MERRY WHEN I HEAR SWEET MUSICK,
FROM 'THE MERCHANT OF VENICE'
Sir John Everett Millais 1829–1896

THE RECONCILIATION OF OBERON AND TITANIA
Sir Joseph Noel Paton 1821–1901

FIRST CLOWN: What is he that builds stronger than either the mason, the shipwright, or the carpenter?
SECOND CLOWN: The gallows-maker; for that frame outlives a thousand tenants.

HAMLET, PRINCE OF DENMARK, ACT 5 SC. 1

Aye me! for aught that I could ever read,
Could ever hear by tale or history,
The course of true love never did run smooth.

A MIDSUMMER NIGHT'S DREAM, ACT 1, SC. 1

ut, damned spot! out, I say! One, two; why then 'tis time to do't. Hell is murky. Fie, my lord, fie! A soldier, and afeard? What need we fear who knows it, when none can call our pow'r to account? Yet who would have thought the old man to have had so much blood in him?

MACBETH, ACT 5, SC. 1

HAMLET
Daniel Maclise 1806–1870

*B*ut be not afraid of greatness. Some are born great, some achieve greatness, and some have greatness thrust upon 'em.

TWELFTH NIGHT; OR, WHAT YOU WILL, ACT 2, SC. 5

T hat which hath made them drunk hath made me bold,
What hath quenched them hath given me fire.

MACBETH, ACT 2, SC. 2

Is this a dagger which I see before me,
The handle toward my hand? Come, let me clutch thee.
I have thee not, and yet I see thee still.
Art thou not, fatal vision, sensible
To feeling as to sight? or art thou but
A dagger of the mind, a false creation,
Proceeding from the heat-oppressed brain?

MACBETH, ACT 2, SC. 1

Under the greenwood tree
Who loves to lie with me,
And turn his merry note
Unto the sweet bird's throat,
Come hither, come hither, come hither.
Here shall he see
No enemy
But winter and rough weather.

AS YOU LIKE IT, ACT 2, SC. 5

LADY MACBETH SLEEPWALKING
Henry Fuseli 1741–1825

False face must hide what
false heart doth know.

MACBETH, ACT 1, SC. 7

Now is the winter of our discontent
Made glorious summer by this sun of York.

KING RICHARD THE THIRD, ACT 1, SC. 1

A horse! a horse!
my kingdom for a horse!

KING RICHARD THE THIRD, ACT 5, SC. 4

THE CHILDREN OF EDWARD IV IN THE TOWER
Paul Delaroche 1797–1856

KING LEAR AND THE FOOL IN THE STORM
William Dyce 1806–1864

This royal throne of kings, this scept'red isle,
This earth of majesty, this seat of Mars,
This other Eden, demi-paradise
This fortress built by Nature for herself
Against infection and the hand of war,
This happy breed of men, this little world
This precious stone set in the silver sea,
Which serves it in the office of a wall,
Or as a moat defensive to a house,
Against the envy of less happier lands...

England, bound in with the triumphant sea,
Whose rocky shore eats back the envious siege
Of wat'ry Neptune, is now bound in with shame,
With inky blots and rotten parchment bonds;
That England, that was wont to conquer others,
Hath made a shameful conquest of itself.

KING RICHARD THE SECOND, ACT 2, SC. 1z

He's mad that trusts in the tameness of a wolf, a
Horse's health, a boy's love, or a whore's oath.

KING LEAR, ACT 3, SC. 6

To be, or not to be – that is the question;
    Whether 'tis nobler in the mind to suffer
The slings and arrows of outrageous fortune,
    Or to take arms against a sea of troubles,
And by opposing end them? To die, to sleep –
    No more; and by a sleep to say we end
The heart-ache and the thousand natural shocks
    That flesh is heir to. 'Tis a consummation
Devoutly to be wish'd. To die, to sleep;
    To sleep, perchance to dream. Ay, there's the rub;
For in that sleep of death what dreams may come,
    When we have shuffled off this mortal coil,
Must give us pause.

HAMLET, PRINCE OF DENMARK, ACT 3, SC. 1

Alas, poor Yorick! I knew him, Horatio: a fellow of infinite
jest, of most excellent fancy; he hath borne me on his
back a thousand times. And now how abhorred in my
imagination it is! My gorge rises at it. Here hung those lips that
I have kiss'd I know not how oft. Where be your gibes now,
your gambols, your songs, your flashes of merriment that were
wont to set the table on a roar? Not one now to mock your
own grinning?

HAMLET, PRINCE OF DENMARK, ACT 5, SC. 1

I must to the barber's, monsieur, for methinks
I am marvellous hairy about the face.

A MIDSUMMER NIGHT'S DREAM, ACT 4, SC. 1

*F*riends, Romans, countrymen, lend me your ears;
I come to bury Caesar, not to praise him.
The evil that men do lives after them;
The good is oft interred with their bones;
So let it be with Caesar. The noble Brutus
Hath told you Caesar was ambitious.
If it were so, it was a grievous fault;
And grievously hath Caesar answer'd it.
Here, under leave of Brutus and the rest –
For Brutus is an honourable man;
So are they all, all honourable men –
Come I to speak in Caesar's funeral.
He was my friend, faithful and just to me;
But Brutus says he was ambitious,
And Brutus is an honourable man.

JULIUS CAESAR, ACT 3, SC. 2

TITANIA AWAKES, SURROUNDED BY ATTENDANT FAIRIES,
CLINGING RAPTUROUSLY TO BOTTOM
Henry Fuseli 1741–1825

Once more unto the breach, dear friends, once more;
    Or close the wall up with our English dead.
In peace there's nothing so becomes a man
    As modest stillness and humility;
But when the blast of war blows in our ears,
    Then imitate the action of the tiger:
Stiffen the sinews, summon up the blood,
    Disguise fair nature with hard-favour'd rage:
Then lend the eye a terrible aspect;
    Let it pry through the portage of the head
Like the brass cannon; let the brow o'erwhelm it
    As fearfully as doth a galled rock
O'erhand and jutty his confounded base,
    Swill'd with the wild and wasteful ocean.
Now set the teeth and stretch the nostril wide;
    Hold hard the breath, and bend up every spirit
To his full height. On, on, you noblest English,
    Whose blood is fet from fathers or war-proof –
Fathers that like so many Alexanders
    Have in these parts from morn till even fought,
And sheath'd their swords for lack of argument.

    KING HENRY THE FIFTH, ACT 3, SC. 1

Why, then the world's mine oyster,
    Which I with sword will open.

THE MERRY WIVES OF WINDSOR, ACT 2, SC. 2

SIR JOHN FALSTAFF
Charles Robert Leslie 1794–1859

THE WITCHES IN MACBETH
Alexander Gabriel Decamps 1803–1860

*D*ouble, double, toil and trouble;
    Fire burn, and cauldron bubble.

Fillet of a fenny snake,
    In the cauldron boil and bake;
Eye of newt, and toe of frog,
    Wool of bat, and tongue of dog,
Adder's fork, and blind-worm's sting
    Lizard's leg, and howlet's wing –
For a charm of pow'rful trouble,
    Like a hell-broth boil and bubble.

Double, double toil and trouble;
    Fire burn, and cauldron bubble.

MACBETH, ACT 4, SC. 1

Romeo, Romeo! wherefore art thou Romeo?
Deny thy father and refuse thy name;
Or, if thou wilt not, be but sworn my love,
And I'll no longer be a Capulet.

ROMEO AND JULIET, ACT 2, SC. 2

Though I look old, yet I am strong and lusty,
For in my youth I never did apply
Hot and rebellious liquors in my blood,
Nor did not with unbashful forehead woo
The means of weakness and debility;
Therefore my age is as a lusty winter,
Frosty, but kindly. Let me go with you;
I'll do the service of a younger man
In all your business and necessities.

AS YOU LIKE IT, ACT 2, SC. 3

ROMEO AND JULIET
Sir Frank Dicksee 1853–1928

MUCH ADO ABOUT NOTHING
Marcus Stone 1840–1921

Friendship is constant in all other things
Save in the office and affairs of love;
Therefore all hearts in love use their own tongues.
Let every eye negotiate for itself,
And trust no agent; for beauty is a witch
Against whose charms faith melteth into blood.

MUCH ADO ABOUT NOTHING, ACT 2, SC. 1

He jests at scars that never felt a wound.
But, soft! What light through
yonder window breaks?
It is the east, and Juliet is the sun.
Arise, fair sun, and kill the envious moon, who is
already sick and pale with grief
That thou her maid art far more fair than she.
Be not her maid, since she is envious;
Her vestal livery is but sick and green,
And none but fools do wear it; cast if off.
It is my lady; O, it is my love!
O that she knew she were!

ROMEO AND JULIET, ACT 2, SC. 2

*S*hall I compare thee to a summer's day?
  Thou art more lovely and more temperate.
Rough winds do shake the darling buds of May,
  And summer's lease hath all too short a date:
Sometime too hot the eye of heaven shines,
  And often is his gold complexion dimm'd,
And every fair from fair some time declines,
  By chance, or nature's changing course, untrimm'd;
But thy eternal summer shall not fade
  Nor lose possession of that fair thou ow'st;
Nor shall Death brag thou wand'rest in his shade,
  When in eternal lines to time thou grow'st.
So long as men can breathe or eyes can see
  So long lives this, and this gives life to thee.

SONNET **XVIII**

SHAKESPEARE READING TO QUEEN ELIZABETH I
John James Chalon 1778–1854

Also in this series
Winston Churchill Quotations

Also available
Little Book of Bath
Little Book of Cambridge
Little Book of Kings & Queens
Little Book of London
Little Book of Oxford

First published in Great Britain in 1997 by
Jarrold Publishing Ltd
Whitefriars, Norwich NR3 1JR

Developed and produced by
The Bridgewater Book Company

Researched and edited by David Notley
Picture research by Vanessa Fletcher

Copyright © 1997 Jarrold Publishing Ltd, latest reprint 2006

Printed and bound in Belgium 5/06
ISBN 13: 978-0-7117-0978-2
ISBN 10: 0-7117-0978-5

Acknowledgements

Jarrold Publishing would like to thank all those who kindly gave
permission to reproduce the words and visual material in this book;
copyright holders have been identified where possible and we
apologise for any inadvertent omissions.

We would particularly like to thank the following
for the use of pictures:
Bridgeman Art Library, Fine Art Photographic Library

Front and back cover: *Shakespeare*, Gerard Soest (*d.* 1861)
Shakespeare Birthplace Trust
Frontispiece: *Ophelia Drowning*, Paul Albert Steck 1895
(Bridgeman Art Library)